A Walk Through Life's Garden

Poems to Motivate and Inspire

Second Edition

By: Jeanette Strachan-Bryson

A WALK THROUGH LIFE'S GARDEN

Copyright © 2014 Jeanette Strachan-Bryson. All Rights Reserved.
ISBN: 978-0-578-15832-7

No part of this book may be reproduced or transmitted in any form or by any means, electronically or printed without permission in writing from the author or publisher.

Printed in the United States of America

Acknowledgements

Sincere appreciations goes out to my late sister- Marjorie, for her input, motivation and wisdom. To my other sisters, Bert, for her expertise and guidance. Ora and Eleanor for their time and assistance. Additional thanks to a host of nieces for their support and encouragements. Special thanks to my number one son, John, for his technical assistance, time and unyielding patience.

Dedication

This book is dedicated to my family, friends, and poetry lovers everywhere. This book is also dedicated to anyone in need of a laugh, a thought provoking message, or a spiritual uplift as they travel along life's pathways.

A Walk Through Life's Garden

Acknowledgements iii
Dedication iv
I. Humorous And Light Hearted Poems 7
   Twenty Second Street 8
   Keep -a- Stepping 10
   The Tongue 11
   Generation X..12
   I AM Retired 13
   Ode to Gossip 14
   Sisters...15
   Cats 16
   A Birthday Acknowledgement 17
   The Poet 18
II. Poems That Tell A Story 19
   Ode to the Apostle Paul 20
   Four Martyred Children 22
   Memories of George, II 24
   The Legend of Fast Man Jim 26
   Lady Wilma 28
   Robert Fulton Brown 29
   What Is a Mother 31
   The Notorious Saul 33
   Fast Man John...35
   Ode to Jackie C. 36
   Hats Off to the Dreamer 37
   Ode to Yesterday 38
   Bring Back the Good Ole Days 39
   Hats Off to the Elderly 40
   Ode to our Senior Citizens..41
III. Inspiration And Grief 42
   Joy Cometh in the Morning 43
   The Dash 45
   Don't Worry, Be Happy 46
   A Political Statement 47
   Wings...48

Risk Taking 49
Forgiveness 50
The Double-Minded Man 51
Exploring Peace and Contentment 52
The Uncertainty of Life 53
Fear 54
Loneliness 55
A Death Wish 56
Be Thankful 57
Memories of Numpy 58
Don't Cry for Me 60

IV. Faith And Reverence 61
Prayer 62
The Final Days 63
God Isn't Finished with Me Yet 64
Only God Knows 65
The Purpose of the Church 66
Be Still 67
A New Creature in Christ 68
Struggling with Sin 70
Religion 71
The Word 72
Dare to Be Different 73
The Comforter 74
Lord, Make Me a Christian 75
My Prayer 76
Onward Christian Soldiers 77
Buckle up for Safety 78
A New Convert 79
Believe in God 80
God is Alive 81
Trust in Jesus 82
You Are the Potter, I Am the Clay 83
Insight 84

I. Humorous And Light Hearted Poems

Twenty Second Street

(Memories of My Childhood and Youth)

We lived in a house on Twenty Second Street
Where everything was quite divine
As children we played and laughed and laughed and Played
and had an extremely good time
Other family members lived nearby and we got
Along just fine
We played kickball regularly, as many young folks did,
And were all of the same mind.

We played games like Hide n Seek, Jump Rope, Simon Says,
and Red Light, our games were full of fun and Adventure
and to everyone's delight
We played a guessing game called "My Riddle, My Riddle,
My Randy Oh" and a musical game where we
All filled in the words to a song
We sang and danced and had lots of fun and we all
Got along just fine

Of course we played Cowboys and Indians as well
And we climbed and jumped out of big trees
When bored we invented new games for fun and Adventure
and everyone played them with ease
As youngsters we had a great passion for poetry and
everyone would read them out loud
Our poems were mostly narratives that we enjoyed as
We entertained the listening crowd

A WALK THROUGH LIFE'S GARDEN

Classical poems we enjoyed reading that left
A glow in our hearts included:
The Charge of the Light Brigade,
The Wreck of the Hesperus, and of course,
The Mills of the Gods.
Other poems enjoyed by us and were a show case for all To
see were: Oh Captain, My Captain, Casey at the Bat, The
Raven, and the ever famous, Annabel Lee

Fun filled activities were enjoyed by all and they were
always pleasant and sweet
We played and joked, and laughed and played and
Enjoyed countless adventures on our own Twenty Second
Street

Keep -a- Stepping

When your performance in life was not up to par
And the world saw you at your worst
So What! Tomorrow is a brand new day
But you must correct your errors first
Then shake the dust off your boots
And gently keep-a- stepping
When your team lost that very important game
And everyone was sad and fretting
Life goes on you know
So shake the dust off your boots
And gently keep-a- stepping
Life experiences consist of all types of encounters
And success is failure turned inside out
We might not win the race every time
And often there are fears and doubts
So let us step high, let us step low
Let's us step to all kinds of musical expressions
When in life you're not at your best, my friend
Just shake the dust off your boots
And gently keep-a- stepping

The Tongue

The tongue is a little instrument
That is powerful but very strong
Allowing some of us to be righteous
While others do much wrong
It is a tiny little member that can cause
Damage, destruction, or bodily harm
Can destroy a man's good name
And make him do much wrong
The tongue has broken up many organizations,
Friendships, and happy homes
Dissolved many partnerships
And its number one ally is the telephone
Man can control the largest ship
When strong winds blow and blow,
By using a tiny instrument called a "Rudder"
That allows ships to go to and fro
The Apostle James tells us that "Man has found a way
To tame the wildest beast, but ways to control the human
Tongue have never been found, offering to some
Much concern but little relief"
If we can just control that little old tongue of ours
Our lives will be in order and complete
By allowing every word uttered to be more wholesome,
Always positive, and sweet

Generation X

The 50's, it was Rock n Roll
The 60's we heard "Stop the war in Vietnam"
The 70's were operation "Parent Search"
A cause that was both interesting and fun
But Generation "X" said they had no cause at all
No reason or cause to fight
No reason to burn their bras or flags
No matter who was wrong or right
But if they would just look around
They would have seen a cause worth fighting for and soon
They too could stop the drugs,
Take a bite out of crime, or have gotten rid of the guns they own
They need not try to change the whole world at one time
They should try to stay down to earth
They have to start with their families, then neighbors, and friends they must make an impact at home first

I AM Retired

No alarm clocks to wake me up
No getting out of bed with much of a fuss
No need to start my day in a great big rush
Why, because I am retired

No more running out of the house with breakfast to go
Grabbing the sports section as I close the door
But relaxing and enjoying the good life I have come to know
because I am retired

I can sleep late if I have no pressing needs
Or start the day reading a newspaper that I retrieved
I can do anything that I darn well please
Why, because I am retired

I can walk my dog or water the lawn
I can go back to bed and sleep until dawn
I can do these things without much of a yawn
Why, because I am now retired

Ode to Gossip

I have broken up many families and friendships
throughout the day. I have started wars and various fights
many times along the way, I am more dangerous
than acid or a gun. When I am in your town
your instincts
better tell you to get-the-stepping, or run
I used to be just a lady's thing, but that was many years ago
Now my entourage consists of men and young children as well
As my fame and notoriety grows
My little brother is known as the "**Little White Lie**"
Of course I am grooming and teaching him well
I am known throughout as "**The Master Destroyer**"
For secrets I will surely tell
I will take a piece from here a piece from there
And the rest I make up you see
The juicer it sounds the larger audience I'll get and
Then more people will cater to me
No man is beyond reproach in fact the rich and famous
Get more of a listening ear
I will make up a situation based on my victims
And will express no remorse or fears
A warning to all my well-wishers, allies, and followers too
Always remember, I have no loyalty to anyone
When my stories are cold and through sizzling
I might just turn on **YOU!!!**

Sisters

Sisters are unique and unpretentious often
Trying to maintain their own identities
Bonded together by DNA, traditions, and customs
Sometimes wanting to shed family values to become
detached and free

Sisters are unique and unpretentious often Expressing
thoughts and opinions without being Asked
They often see the dark side of their siblings' Friends and
loved ones and will do their best to
Reveal that person's hidden past

Sisters are unique and unpretentious and are truly
A gift from God
They are sometimes each other's number one Confidant and
will keep their sister's secret close at heart

My own sisters are unique and unpretentious and Have
been for oh so long
We laugh and joke and will not always agree but I am so
glad they are mine

Cats

A cat is a finicky animal
With a mind of its own
Cannot be prompted or conjured
Or seldom taught new skills at home
A cat is a bundle of fur and joy
To cat lovers every where
They try hard to maintain good grooming skills
Even though they might shed their own hair
A cat is a good judge of character
So give special attention to its dislikes
It might one day come back to haunt you
By causing you much pain and strife
A cat is a loyal feline who will stand by you
Until the end
Once he realizes he can trust you
And that you are truly his friend
Cats are stubborn little creatures
But oh, so very smart
They are adorable when they are little kittens
And will capture most anyone's heart
They walk around with an air of boldness
And superiority
But after having gained your confidence
And trust
They are as humble as can be
I love the little felines
Because they are as cute as can be
They will curl at the foot of your bed at night
Providing a feeling of inner peace and tranquility

A Birthday Acknowledgement

Who is that person that's around about
Spreading happiness and joy inside out
She has a heart of gold and there is no doubt
She is our own precious Martha

Who loves to sew, cook, and bake
Can turn out a designer's apron
Or bake a number one cake
She can bake a honey roasted ham
Without much wait
She is our own precious Martha

Who loves the Lord and her family too
But has even more love for me and you
She shows it each day the whole year through
She is our own precious Martha

So on this day our wish for you is to
Celebrate and make a wish or two
We are all here today because we love
And cherish you

Happy Birthday Multifaceted Martha!!!

The Poet

She enjoy all kinds of poetry—
Like Longfellow, Kaplan, and Guest
Poems that told a story were her favorite ones
Where morals and values are expressed
She then tried to get into the authors' head
To find out what he was all about
And tried hard to envision what thoughts he wanted conveyed
And which ones he wanted to do without
She then began to memorize one line at a time
Once perfected she move on to another
She then said each line the way the author
Would have wanted them expressed
Try this and you too will be richly blessed

II. Poems That Tell A Story

Ode to the Apostle Paul

The Apostle Paul was once a heartless man
Who persecuted many followers of Christ
But after having had that, now famous "Damascus Experience"
He made a complete change within his life
After becoming converted he became a good
Foot soldier for Christ
He said "As a good solider we must endure hardship
But should never entangle ourselves with the affairs of this life"
He was a mentor to other Christians
And gave words of wisdom far and near
He was an apostle, a preacher, a writer and a teacher
Spreading God's word everywhere
He admonished them to be strong in faith
Study God's word and keep it near
For it would give you love peace and happiness but not that of fear
He kept churches intact
By sending them letters on situations close at hand
Giving them solutions, advice and consolations needed
To the various churches throughout the land
He was also a mentor to young pastors
Bishops and deacons everywhere
Reminding them to study, to show thyself approved
And to show others that they care
He inspired them with the word of God
And effectively spread his knowledge throughout the land

Encouraging evangelists to preach the word in and out of season
And make God known to every man
In Paul's final days he urged them all to "be strong in faith"
And to do the things that are right
For he had labored long and hard
And indeed had fought a good fight
As we journey through life, we too should seek to acquire
That now famous "Damascus Experience"
And make it the ultimate adventure in our lives
So that we too may enjoy peace and happiness
With our Lord and Savior, Jesus Christ

A WALK THROUGH LIFE'S GARDEN

Four Martyred Children

(Memories of Four Young Girls Who Died in
a Church Bombing)

Four young Black girls who just happened to be at
The right place the wrong day and at the wrong time
All bursting with youthful zest and energy and with
A head full of hope, aspirations, and dreams of things
To come

Never imagining that going to church that Sunday would be
their last day on earth
Never imagining that breakfast would be the last meal
They ate, never imagining that Sunday School would be the
last time to socialize with church friends
And never imagining that on that day their life on earth
would end

Because of their untimely tragedy the world is now Denied
of prospective doctors, lawyers, teachers and Such, a
senseless act that was by far too much
Their families and community were robbed of daughters,
Sisters, classmates and friends
Never imagining that this is how their lives would end

September 15, 1963 was the day, the bombing of the
Sixteenth Street Church went down in history
Many said it was wrong and did not have to be, but
God knew this was needed for all the world to see
In order to bring about compassion and to show some

A WALK THROUGH LIFE'S GARDEN

Sympathy

Bombings are ever present during times of war but to Bomb
a church killing little children was just the last Straw
Often explosives serve a needed purpose, and bought their
Inventor fortune and fame
It wasn't intended to bomb a building causing innocent
Children suffering and pain

The bomber's energy could have been used to spread a little
peace and goodwill
But not to cause needless pain and suffering by Destroying a
church where innocent children were killed

Many questioned the character of the men who did such
A terrible thing
Their only concern was to bomb a church building and To
spread hatred to every wing

The four little girls are now at peace because their death
Was not in vain
They have touched the lives of many and will be
Remembered with love, sweetness and yes, even pain

Memories of George, II

(A tribute to my nephew)
He was the third of six children plus one
And was his parents' pride and joy
You see after having had two lovely little girls
This child would be their first baby boy
And, oh what a beautiful baby, and he was
Given his father's first name
He was said to be a "very lucky" child for he had
Cheated fate many times at its own game
He grew up to be a pleasant young lad and got
Along with everyone it seemed
He was often funny, had a good sense of humor
And no one could say he was ever mean
For a while he was a single parent raising a daughter alone
Until the lovely Andrea came into his life
Making his house a real home
Together they added two more children to the fold
Making a total of three
He was a good provider and a family man
And was just as humble as he could be
He was kind-hearted and generous
And told the best jokes in town
Never seeking pity from anyone
Even when he was sick or down
One day God looked around at his garden
And thought it was not quite completed
So he plucked a tender Rose from the Adam's vineyard
For he knew that was just what he needed

A WALK THROUGH LIFE'S GARDEN

We will miss his laughter, his jokes, and his acts of generosity
But we can take comfort that we knew him
As he passed through this life
For indeed he was a true friend to both you and me

The Legend of Fast Man Jim

(A Tribute to My Dad, James Melvin Strachan)

He had the speed that many desire
A fast man for many, many years
He often referred to himself as a "minute man"
Because he was so fast at getting around town
They said he was so fast you couldn't throw water on him
Of course that was a mere exaggeration
But he was number one in his group and this needed no explanation
He was a big man whom everyone respected
And was always referred to by his full name
His temper was high but he never got into fights
Causing no man problems or shame
He was not one to ever sleep late in bed
And he arose at the crack of dawn
"Always rise before day clean" he would say
Meaning very early in the morn
He never tolerated nonsense
And was thought by many to be mean
But he had the heart of gold and gave willingly to any man
Expecting no returns to be seen
He had a head for numbers
A calculator he was always without
As he added large columns of numbers in his head
And they were always right; beyond any shadow of a doubt
He believed in saving his money
Had money in as many as four different banks in town

A WALK THROUGH LIFE'S GARDEN

"Save a dime out of every dollar" he would say
With a dollar, you are never broke or down
He was a man of means about town and he taught his children well
He told them "Real Estate is a piece of the rock
But don't ever borrow or sell"
He built his home with his own hands
Where he lived for over fifty years
Fond memories we all had in that house
Where many family activities were held
Years had taken their toll on him
And this fast man had slowed down some
He walks very slowly with a cane
And his mind is no longer sharp and keen
His hearing is gone and he said his eyes run water
Like "Jerry Burgus"
And arthritis is a constant thorn in his side
But fond memories of happy events
Stand firm within his heart
So friends let's not dwell on the negative
Rather let's keep past memories within our hearts
Of fast man Jim and his memories
A man who was once big, strong, fast and smart

A WALK THROUGH LIFE'S GARDEN

Lady Wilma

(Memories of Hurricane Wilma in Florida)

We all knew she was coming, but
Underestimated her strength
She was swift and unpredictable during her visit
Leaving a bill way over a mint

We all took the necessary precautions
Like food, water, and drinks
But Wilma arrived very early that morning
We were not fully awake and had little time to think

She was thought by many to be a tornado
As she damaged and destroyed things in her way
Uprooting trees and large structures and caused
Us all to have a rather unsafe and soggy day

Her strength intensified as she traveled to various
Cities throughout the state of Florida
Knocking out our source of electricity, causing us
To use candles, lamps, and to boil drinking water

Andrew, Donna, and Charley were bad but to me
None was as bad as she. Many had no electricity for two
weeks or more while others chose to flee

In spite of Wilma's activities the damage, death total
And personal injuries were down to a few
We should count it all joy when experiencing situations
Such as this then ask God for strength and guidance to see
us through

Robert Fulton Brown

(A kindly old neighbor of my childhood)

He enjoyed playing checkers
Was the best domino player in town
Card playing was a cinch for him
That good ole Robert Fulton Brown.
He mastered the sport of fishing
And would catch a fish or two with ease
He was an elderly gentleman about town
Always aiming to please
He always had a pleasant smile on his face
And was kind and gentle as can be
A hat he was never seen without
Which he used to tip to the ladies
As he traveled about
The children all adored him
And they called him" Papa Brown"
The yearly parties he gave for them
Were always the best in town
He had the most beautiful garden
That you ever did see
And he unselfishly shared them
With anyone and for any
Occasion it seemed

A WALK THROUGH LIFE'S GARDEN

He was the pillar of his community
Who would give to any cause
And he always put the good Master first
As his trusted Savior and Lord
He generously donated to many charities
Like hospitals colleges and such
Was on the board of countless committees
But always had time to give to others that special touch
Robert Fulton Brown is no longer with us
But his legend lingers on
"Never owe any man a penny", he would say
And always let your word be your bond

A WALK THROUGH LIFE'S GARDEN

What Is a Mother

(A Tribute to My Mother, Elmore W. Strachan)

A mother is one who would
Comfort her children and do her
Best to make the hurt better
Would stand by them through
Good and bad or any kind of weather
A mother is one who would love and support her children
And never neglect their needs
She would do her best to enrich their lives
In hopes that they would succeed
A mother is one who knows her children inside and out
Can motivate and inspire them by casting out
Their fears and doubts
She knows their strengths and weaknesses
Their limitations and abilities
Knows how to instill confidence in them
As she helps them hurdle over life's
Turbulence and victories
A mother is one who is smart enough to reserve her comments
And instead of saying: "Oh, no, not my child,"
Will quietly do her own investigation
Then handle it with grace and style
She teaches her children of God

A WALK THROUGH LIFE'S GARDEN

And of his undying love
And reminds them of his gift
To them that was sent from heaven above
She builds up a spiritual foundation in them
And fills it up with great tools
Like morals, values, and wisdom
And then she tosses in the golden rule
A mother indeed is lots of things to her children
Who truly love her
Many women can birth children
But it takes a special woman to be a Mother

A WALK THROUGH LIFE'S GARDEN

The Notorious Saul

Saul was a blasphemer, persecutor, and an insolent man
Who had no heart, conscience, or creed
He persecuted Christians out of ignorance and unbelief
Making his mark in Satan's world for his notorious
Acts and immoral deeds
He was a Pharisee and a tent maker by trade
Who persecuted Christians everywhere
He participated in the stoning of Stephen
And tore down churches far and near
Then lo and behold a miraculous experience
He had on a road one day
Made a tremendous impact on him as it turned his life around
Making him over the Christian way
It temporarily blinded him as it prepared him for his life anew
He was thoroughly purged inside out
And was made clean through and through
God knew that Saul was his chosen instrument
Who would experience suffering for his name
So he was given a new heart, a new name, a new life
And an opportunity to be redeemed
Without any guilt or shame
The joy of salvation was implanted in his heart
As well as love, meekness, long suffering, and grace
He was given a new position among men
As God prepared him for daily encounters to face
For many years he traveled around teaching and preaching
God's Word far and near

A WALK THROUGH LIFE'S GARDEN

He served as a mediator to help churches settle disputes
And trained new converts everywhere
He fought the good fight, finished his course
And left behind inspiring words to give us
wisdom and strength
He encouraged all Christians to press onward to meet the
mark
Forgetting those things behind, always striving onward for
more souls to win.

Fast Man John

(A Tribute to My Son)
He was the grandson of fast man Jim and
Displayed that same physical physique
He was tall and handsome, big and strong
And would not lie down to accept defeat

He was an entrepreneur about town, trying
To employ the wisdom of fast man Jim
Once a sheepskin in business was obtained
He knew success would not be readily grim

He equipped himself with knowledge and internalized the
wisdom of his predecessor
Before him
Trying hard to create the replica of that ever
Famous fast man Jim

He tried his luck at being a salesman and
Everyone was impressed by his charm
He was successful yet humble and swiftly moved
Around town earning him the name "Fast Man John"

He was successful at his sales (many on the internet)
While working a regular job from nine to five
He learned how to market and sell his products and
How to be thrifty yet wise

He is grateful to his predecessor for having passed down wisdom and knowledge to him and thankful for a discerning spirit that encouraged him to follow in the footsteps of that ever famous Fast Man Jim.

A WALK THROUGH LIFE'S GARDEN

Ode to Jackie C.

(A Tribute to a Retired School Teacher)

Every now and then someone enters our lives
And touches our hearts in a very special way
They might have given us words of wisdom, good
Sound advice, or may have brighten up our day

For some of us this person might have been Ann Landers,
Mother Teresa, Dr. King, or countless
Wannabes
But I know a person who is remarkable in every sense
Of the word, and she is the modest Jackie C.

Now Jackie C. is what you call a God fearing women Who is
compassionate, caring, and helpful in every way
She is patient, kind, and cheerful and does her best to help
someone each and every day

She is a teacher, nurse, and a lawyer always willing to
Give her very best
She is a mentor, missionary, wife, and a mother putting
aside little time to rest

Although now retired from her profession as an educator
Where she shaped the minds of many children in her Care
She will now wear new serving hats (but will keep Her
Teaching one as well) as she continues spreading Joy to
everyone far and near

Hats Off to the Dreamer

(A Tribute to Dr Martin Luther King)

The dreamer dreamed of a better world
One filled with peace and of harmony
Where everyone got along quite well
And enjoyed each other's company
The dreamer dreamed of a better world
Where one's color was obsolete
A world where a person's character and the contents
Of his heart would be given top priority
The dreamer dreamed of a world where ignorance,
Prejudice, and hatred would be declared
Negative connotations and be thrown out
Of our lives, our hearts, our world
And be erased from our present memory
The dreamer dreamed of many things
That would enrich the lives of you and me
He shared his dreams with everyone
In hopes that this world would
Be better for all to see

Ode to Yesterday

Gone are the days of the extended family
That served as eyes, ears, and shoulders to lean on
In times of sadness and misery
Gone are the days when grandma and grandpa
Were not far away in the next town
But were close enough to comfort the family
Through life's turmoil and everyday frowns
Gone are the days when history, wisdom, and knowledge
Were passed down first hand indeed
And learning about past history was even
Better than watching TV
Gone are the days
When experience would not have been questioned
Rather it was used as a precautionary measure or guiding
force to mention
Gone are the days when a verbal agreement closed a deal
And there was never a need for lawyers or contracts
Because everyone was honest and for real
Yes these days are gone and passed
And are never to be seen again
For they are lost and gone forever
But their memories should be kept in our hearts
As we move on to make things better

Bring Back the Good Ole Days

I was setting down by my window
Staring at the breezy trees
Reminiscing about days of old and how it used to be
When a man's word was his bond
And a handshake settled it all
And every effort was made to repay a debt
No matter how large or small
When fighting at school was limited
To putting up your dukes to fight
And guns were never, never used
No matter who was wrong or right
There were no drug problems (so to speak)
The word "**Getting High**" was not coined yet
The homeless were in such small numbers
That a name for them had not been set
Values and morals were at an all-time high
While promiscuity was at an all-time low
Juvenile Delinquency was in such small numbers
Yes these are the days I missed so

Hats Off to the Elderly

Hats off to the elderly
This group deserves respect
For having kept their families together
Without any hesitations or regrets
Hats off to the elderly
They have withstood many of life's tests
Having led and guided us through much turmoil
And always gave their best
Hats off to the elderly
Who has molded and shaped our country well
Using God as a guiding force
Their efforts never failed
Hats off to the elderly
Who have proven to be an example for us all
For without their knowledge and expertise
We would have truly indeed be lost

Ode to our Senior Citizens

They say age is but a number
And if this phase is so
Our elderly should be honored
For the wealth of knowledge they know
If age is but a number
An employer should jump with joy
For the added years of expertise
A senior citizen could employ
If age is but a number
Then our families will be blessed
For the years of the elderly wisdom
And experience that would withstand many of life's tests
If age is but a number
Society should make it perfectly clear
That our loved ones must not be devalued
While they can still do their share
As mentors, foster grandparents, or consultants
To a needed soul here and there
If age is but a number
The thought must be made perfectly clear
Our elderly must be treated with dignity and respect
We must cherish and hold them dear

III. Inspiration And Grief

Joy Cometh in the Morning

Are you currently going through a storm
And just can't seem to find your way through
Remember:
Joy cometh in the morning
And God will take care of you
Are you unhappy with your job
Because it appears as if others
Have gotten promoted
Or rewarded with ease
Remember:
Joy cometh in the morning
For this thought is refreshing and is sure to please
When your bills are at an all-time high
And your finances are at an all-time low
Keep the thought:
Joy cometh in the morning
Even though the pace
May be exceedingly slow
When you are in a desperate situation
And you are pressed against the wall
Remember:
Joy cometh in the morning
No matter how hard you might fall
When your family relationships are not

What they should be
Forgiveness and reconciliation are moving slow
Keep the thought:
Joy cometh in the morning
And believe in your heart it is so
When life turns its back on you
And friends' promises have fallen through
Keep the thought:
Joy cometh in the morning
For this phrase is simple, but true
"Joy Cometh in the Morning"

A WALK THROUGH LIFE'S GARDEN

The Dash

(April 12, 1960 – January 18, 2009)

Man's earthly existence extends from
The cradle to the grave
Filled with achievements and disappointments
And many things along the way

The Dash is the linking force that to some
Is a point of brevity
Allowing us to bridge the gap from our earthly
Existence to eternity

There were those who during their lifetime
Had success; good health, family and friends
While others traveled through life thinking
Of things that could have been

We must grab life by the bootstraps and then
Attempt smooth sailing straight ahead
We must fill it with our own "Bucket List"
Before moving on to the next stage

A "Bucket List" consists of all the things in life
That you want to do
Before ending one phase of your life
And going on to phase two

We must do things that are noteworthy
So we can leave a legacy or two
We must make an impression before leaving this Earth so
others can say something good about you

Don't Worry, Be Happy

(Matthew 6: 25-34)

Worry is an endless task we should try to do without
It diminishes our assertiveness, and replaces it
With fears and doubts
It chips away at our self-esteem as it crushes our
Confidence and power
Denying us of much needed sleep for many countless hours
Worry can alter our health status
By causing the body mental anguish and bodily pain
It can diminish our social status by affecting
Our financial losses and gains
The "**Word**" tells us not to worry about life
Or about what we eat, drink or wear
But to go to our heavenly father
For he knows just how much we can bear.
The birds in the sky never worry
About what they will eat from day to day
Because they know that their heavenly father will
Provide for them in a very special way
The lilies in the field never worry about clothes
Yet they are always richly dressed
For they know that their heavenly father provides for them
Ensuring that they are properly clothed and always at their
best We must first seek the kingdom of God and his
righteousness
And other things will come to pass for our father in heaven
loves
Us and will provide for us, First Class! So let's not worry about
tomorrow for each day has enough trouble of its own
Let us **live, enjoy life** and **be happy**! Our heavenly father is
still on the throne

A Political Statement

They say it is politically incorrect to openly express your views
The end result might not always be to your advantage
May even cost you a friend or two
They say it is politically incorrect to be different
Stand out or deviate from the norm
It may cost you that promotion,
A seat on the board, or even bodily harm
They say it is politically incorrect to discuss religion or politics
With people you don't know
It may limit your chances of fortune or fame
By hindering your ability to grow
Politically incorrect is any thought, action, or deed
Deemed inappropriate by society
And held to the highest esteem by the majority
A politically correct statement is based simply on the trend of time
May even change from day to day without any reason,
Cause, or rhyme.
We should base our thoughts and opinions on Bible doctrines
That do not change from day to day
It would open our minds and unclog our thoughts
Allowing us to think more clearly the Christian way

Wings

Our children are our offspring, they are ours
From the cradle to the grave
We must nurture them with kindness
As they go along life's way
We must mold and shape them
And not give up if they fail
Our children are our future
We are the wind beneath their sail
Our children need our guidance and training to succeed
We must teach them to be productive
In their every act and deed
We must help them to develop their strengths and abilities
And encourage them to do their very best
In their triumphs and victories
Our children are a mere extension of all of us
We must develop in them good character
Based on morals values and trust
And lay down the groundwork
For them to succeed, not to fail
Our children are our future
We are the wind beneath their sail

Risk Taking

They say it is important to take a risk
In every day situations
You might not always get good results
But the outcome may be favorable on many occasions
They say it's important to take a risk
Step out on faith as one might say
So stick to that idea, if it makes sense to you
And go through with it all the way
What if Columbus had not taken that risk
And became filled with frustrations and despair?
Our history books would be altered
To say that the earth was square
And what if the pilgrims had not taken that risk
To venture out on their own
We would all be living under the British flag
Worshipping as one
And what if the Wright brothers had a vision
But failed to act on it?
There would be no such thing as an Airplane,
Helicopter, Space Ship, or a Super Jet
If a risk wasn't taken we might have never known
If we would have succeeded or failed
And many inventions that we use today
would have been to no avail
Risk taking is good, risk taking is smart
Risk taking is an opportunity to allow us to develop our
Thoughts, exploring new and perhaps better possibilities
So as we venture through life
Let us continue to discover, explore, or take a risk or two
For it might make us rich and famous by opening up doors
for you

Forgiveness

Unforgiveness is a negative term that may burden us down
With hardship and strife
Hinders our ability to move on and may even prevent
Us from doing our best in life
When done wrong by others, and revenge
Seems to be the best thing to do
We must practice self-discipline by turning the other cheek
As God has instructed us to do
He will cast down his wrath and deal with the situation in time
He will take away our burden and give us peace of mind
When asked how many times should our enemies be forgiven
Christ replied not one, two, or three times
But seventy times seven
There may be some who would go out of their way
To attack your opinion and good name
We are humans so it's only natural
That we feel threatened, burdened, and pained
But Christ said to forgive others as he has forgiven you
It's often hard to be humble, but it is the right thing to do
So we should forgive our brothers then move on with our lives
If we let God handle it, it would free our minds of
Mental anguish and mind-boggling strife

The Double-Minded Man

A double-minded man is without rhyme, reason
Style, shape, or form
He swings to either side of the pendulum
With an attitude that is carefree and calm
He usually sides with the majority
Rejecting what is right
Putting aside his innermost thoughts
Always trying to avoid a fight
Jacob compared Reuben to water
Meaning he was unstable without any shape, style, or form
Water would take the shape of its container
Whether cylinder, square, rectangle, or round
The Apostle James tells us that a double-minded man
Is unstable in all his ways
He is like the waves of the sea
Tossing to and fro for never ending days
The "Word" tells us not to be lukewarm
But to be either hot or cold
We must take a stand, step up to the bat
And become **Outrageously** bold
We must be committed, stop straddling the fence
And take a stand for Christ
Never minding what the world might say
We must do the things that are right

Exploring Peace and Contentment

As you go throughout the day you should
Do some things to spread a little
Sunshine and to brighten up the day
First you should thank God for giving you
Another day on this earth
And if you show it in your acts and deeds it would add to your sense of worth

Next establish a personal goal that is Needed by you
Nothing very fancy or very hard to do
Aim for the stars and with persistence
You will reach it in time
And if by chance you reach the moon Consider it all just fine

You should seek beautiful things that we
Ignore every day like a colorful butterfly, a Beautiful flower, or a humming bird that Might pass your way
Then look for traits of beauty in folks you See each day, like a warm smile, a gentle Spirit, or a positive attitude they might Display

Lastly you should think positive thoughts And look for people of the same mind
Keep a song in your heart, be kind to others, and be assured that your peace and Contentment will flow like wine

The Uncertainty of Life

Life is a mere uncertainty as you go from day to day
Filled with joy, sorrow, and many things along the way
You should leap out on faith and throw caution to the wind
Taking a risk at any course and always believing that you can
Our life does not always work out according to our plans
Rejections, disappointments, and heartaches are plentiful
And very often close at hand
When stepping out on faith
To assume that much needed task
You should always consult the higher power above
For directions, instructions, and inner strength
For He can halt your very first step
Or send you smooth sailing straight ahead
We should always put Him first in our lives
As we draw new strength each day
So live life to the fullest
And dare to take a risk or two
For life indeed is an uncertainty my friends
But faith, endurance, and a positive attitude
Will see you through

Fear

Fear is an old dark monster that lives within us all
Causing us to resist taking a risk, no matter how large or small
It causes us to have nightmares
And to be awakened for countless hours
It may even strip us of our reasoning ability
And rob us of our energy and power
It can "zap" the strength out of any saint
And bring a big man to his knees
May weaken the roars of any lion
As it overpowers them with ease
Fear has made the biggest of men break out in a cold sweat
And has made the boldest of women
Quiver and shake until her hands were wet
Fear can make a baby cry out for its mom
As it's terrorized many youngsters
Making them think the dark will do them harm
Fear is many things to all of us and makes us act in such a way
That it clouds our minds with uncertainties
As it overtakes us from day to day
We can overpower this old monster if we confront it face to face
And replace it with common sense and faith
We will be sure to win this race

Loneliness

Loneliness is like a river that goes on and on
Never ceasing to renew its strength as it
Flows on to catch the morning dawn
Loneliness is like the midnight
Dark, cold and wet
Offering little comfort to anyone
Showing much pain and regret
Loneliness is like a shadow that creeps alongside of you
Clouding your pathway with darkness
As it adds to your feelings of gloominess and blue
Loneliness is like the earth as it rotates
Round and round and round
Changing your state from day to night
As it turns your joys into frowns.
Loneliness is being alone in a crowd
No matter how large or small
Feelings of misery and isolation creeps in
And you wish not to have been there at all

A Death Wish

The old man walked down the street at
His slow and unsteady pace
Staring at familiar scenes and
At some unfamiliar faces
Reminiscing about days of old
And how it used to be
Thinking of days long passed and
Of his sweet Emily

It's been one year since she left this earth
One year seems like eternity
One year of sadness, emptiness
And pain was his thoughts daily
He longed for the day when he too
Could step over to the other side
And never be sad or lonely again
As he graciously enters the rim in the sky

Be Thankful

When enjoying yourself at a ballgame or other events of the day
We often become frustrated when others stand in our way
But we should count our blessings
Even though the situation may seem a little blight
In spite of it all we should take comfort in knowing that
We have our precious eyesight
When your transportation becomes a problem
Causing you to do a little walking in the heat
Instead of complaining give thanks to God that
You can still walk on your own two feet
When doing chores like mowing the lawn
Ironing clothes or bringing groceries into the house
We should continuously be thankful for our limbs
That enables us to move all about
Every now and then
A challenge enters into our life to test our faith
As we endure turmoil and momentary strife
So when obstacles are placed in our lives
We need not feel sad or blue
Just thank God anyway
Next ask for strength to endure
For He surely will see you through

Memories of Numpy

(A Tribute to My Niece at Her Untimely Death)

She was a tower of strength to everyone, she was
Brave, courageous, and bold
She struggled and battled with that childhood illness of
Hers but she never gave up as I was told

You see, she was diagnosed as a Juvenile Diabetic at The
tender age of ten
She never sought favoritism or pity from anyone as she
Went through life, her goal was to conquer that ole enemy
and win

She had a pleasing personality with a warm and radiant
smile
She was never grumpy or complained, she tackled each new
day with grace and style

Numpy loved little children, she enjoyed playing with them,
reading to them, and teaching them new songs
She would wipe their tears, she listened to their problems as
she encouraged them to learn new things and be strong

She had a genuine love for her family and always put her
family first
She taught by example as she showed compassion and
forgiveness to everyone no matter how bad her feelings
might have been hurt

A WALK THROUGH LIFE'S GARDEN

Today there is a definite void in our hearts, but Numpy did
what she had to do
She left us a legacy of peace, love, kindness and forgiveness
for all of us to follow, for indeed these traits will see us
through

Don't Cry for Me

Don't cry for me, for you know I was just passing Through
My task here has ended and there is nothing more to do
Don't cry for me for I feel no pain or distress
I have shed this earthly body and have gone home to Take my rest

Don't cry for me for I have been looking forward to this Trip for a while
I yearn to see friends and loved ones who have gone Before
And will greet them with a smile

Don't cry for me, rather treasure precious memories left behind
Lock them in your heart and treasure them until we Meet at another time

IV. Faith And Reverence

Prayer

Prayer to God is something you should strive to do
More and more each day
No formalities or expertise are needed, you just
Talk to him in your own special way
The family prayer was a classic in days of old
It bonded the family together and gave food and
Nourishment for the soul
The prayers of the elderly projected a special touch
And the Bible tells us that "The effectual, fervent prayer
Of the righteous availeth much"
You should not pray openly as the Pharisees did in days
Of old, but should find your own special chambers
That only you and God knows
And if you pray in the secret chambers that God had
Spoken, your heavenly father would answer your prayers
And graciously reward you in the open
You should pray without ceasing and openly rejoice
If you pray morning, evening, and noontime your
Heavenly Father would hear your voice
You should pray during the good times and pray during the
bad
You should pray when you are happy, and pray when you are
Sad. You should continuously pray the whole day
Through, a mere simple prayer to God will open doors for
you
So upon returning home in the evenings after a long and
busy Day, it will fill your heart with gladness if you just
remember to pray

The Final Days

Our World today is a disaster
Evidence of this can be seen everywhere
Children are obsessed with firearms
And use real guns without any fears
Floods and droughts are in our cities
While terrorist bombs are far and near
Our days on earth are coming to a closure
As prophesies in Matthew 24 are being fulfilled
Wars, rumors of wars, and false prophets
Are visible and present in every way
While famines, pestilence, and earth quakes
Are in diverse places and in our cities and towns today
Our children are smarter, the economy is stronger
And inventions are flourishing everyday
Men are wiser, women are more independent
And many are just too busy to pray
We have more material gains, bigger houses, and better jobs
But some of us work from dawn to dusk, ignoring Christ and
our Families for profit and expensive cars
Surely we are living in the last days; proof of this can be
seen Everywhere, but there is hope for a better tomorrow
One without sickness, pain, or fear
Time is winding down as our days on earth come to an end,
so get your house in order for our Lord and Savior is coming
back again, change your lifestyle, grow strong in faith by
reading your
Bible everyday, our world is a disaster, we must stay in the
word and pray!

God Isn't Finished with Me Yet

If in the course of our conversation
I made you really lose your wit
Please be patient with me
God isn't finished with me yet
If my actions caused you pain and strife
Or harsh words caused you to fret
Please be patient with me
God isn't finished with me yet
If promises made fell through
Causes you much heartache and regret
Please be patient with me
God isn't finished with me yet
Once a person becomes a new Christian in Christ
And starts life anew
Old habits accumulated over the years
Do not just disappear to one or two
As a person becomes a new creature in Christ
And begins to do the things that are right
One by one, old habits will leave him
It might take weeks, months, years, but seldom over night
Yes I am a new creature in Christ
Struggling hard to pass the daily test
So please please be patient with me
For God isn't finished with me yet

Only God Knows

Only God knows our many heartaches
Our suffering loss and pain
He knows when to give assistance
And when to step back and not intervene
He knows our many frustrations
Our hopelessness and despair
Sometimes we may feel within our hearts
That He just doesn't care
And sometimes we may feel that we
Are totally left alone
As we struggle to unravel life's puzzles
And get out of the maze boxes on our own
But he steps back time and time again
As He looks over our shoulders
Giving us the opportunity to grow
And become one of His soldiers
We all have experienced times
When we felt there was no way out
When suddenly an idea came to us
(That was God beyond any shadow of a doubt)
Sometimes the small things we may take for granted
But God continues to bless us in spite
Of our many disenchantments
So when we experience a loss
Confronted with insurmountable problems
Or feeling miserable and blue
Just remember God's grace and mercy
Will always see you through!

The Purpose of the Church

The church is more than just a building
Where good preaching and music are heard
And more than a reception center
Where one can be entertained by God's Word
It is a training ground for soldiers
As stated in Matthew 28:19-20:
We are commissioned to baptize and make disciples out of men
Encouraging them to spread "The Good News" to many

Another purpose of the church is found in Ephesians 4:12:
It is to edify or build up the soul
So that we may become better Christians
Indeed the church is more than a building
Where good preaching and music are heard
After obtaining a Christian education
We must move on to spread God's Word

Be Still

As you travel down the road of life and
Experience problems far and near
The word tells us to stop, take time to meditate
For God will never put more on us than we can bear
When facing a dilemma with an approaching deadline near
The word tells us to put our trust in God
Ask for guidance then sit back and be still

When confronted with various obstacles that we
Cannot afford to delay
The word tells us to be still, God will fight our battles
But we must trust him and obey
SO STOP! WAIT! AND BE PERFECTLY STILL!
To await God's answer and to consistently do his will

A WALK THROUGH LIFE'S GARDEN

A New Creature in Christ

Religion is the bold thing today
To be saved is to be popular, cool or hip
Many of us are playing the follow the leader game
And we are in and out of religion real quick
Once a person has been born again, and becomes a
New person in Christ, he should give up his old ways
But must begin to do all the things that are right
To go around ranting and raving is not the wisest thing to do
For once you become a new creature in Christ
Others will see the change in you
When you become born again your life becomes brand new
You no longer want, need, or desire to do the things you used to do
Accepting Christ and changing your life are only the first
Steps, you know, but once you have mastered
Those much-needed steps you must be ready
To move and grow
A new creature should next develop a strong
Love for Jesus in his every act and deed
He should show it, share it, and live it
In the kind of life he leads
He should next love the Bible, and read it every day
Feed upon it, digest, and accept it in each and every way
He should love his brothers and sisters in Christ
Even though they might sometimes hurt him
Or may not always do the things that are right
Next he should try to love his enemies, to some
This may be a hard thing to do

But God said: "Love ye one another as I have loved you"
Lastly he should love to talk to God and worship him
In praise and song
This would keep him from straying away and from
Doing things that are wrong
So becoming a Christian is more than having a
Religious experience and just leaving it all there
It is changing your whole lifestyle, gaining knowledge of
Christ, and spreading God's word far and near

Struggling With Sin

(Romans 7: 8-25)

From time to time in our lives, we occasionally go through a test
As we travel through life's journey, trying hard to do our best
Sin seizes this opportunity to create in us all sorts of desires
We then become perplexed and confused,
Not wanting to do what we want to do
But rather led by demonic thoughts that have been inspired

It's that sinful nature inside that often channels
And directs this life of mine
Spearheading and prompting my inner most thoughts
And leading me most of the time

As I reflect on my life as a "Wretched Man"
I wonder how could I escape this living death?
I then delight in God's words
That are powerful and strong
For it's comforting to know
It will bring us peace, joy, and a sense of rest

Religion

Religion has been a refuge in days of old
It healed the heart when it was heavy
And was food and nourishment for the soul
Our country was built on religion
Religious freedom was our forefather's greatest need
They wanted to live in a country
Where they could worship God as they please
Religion was very important to our country
Its ideologies and practices were such,
Currencies were printed with the inscriptions
Printed boldly: "**In God We Trust**"
The pledge of allegiance stated
Without even sparing the rod
That this country's allegiance
Would be under the guidance of God
A daily ritual observed in schools everywhere
Was to openly acknowledge God in prayer
As children strived to be educated
In a classroom without guns or fear
During periods of slavery and bondage
Religion was important to our ancestors
As they went about their daily lives
It gave new hope to the hopeless, and strength
To those whose days often consisted of turmoil and strife
For many, religion has lost its great impact and
Its practice is believed to be for the very old
But we must continuously focus on it
For its principles are greater than silver or gold

The Word

The Word will comfort you when needed
Lift you up when you're feeling low
Build up your self-esteem as it helps
You to grow and grow and grow
It has been said to "broaden your horizon"
And give light to those who entertain it
Will make any man wiser and
Give understanding to even the simple
The Bible tells us: "Happy is the man who entertains
The Word in his thoughts"
For God's Word is said to be quick and powerful
And sharper than any double edged sword
Faith comes by hearing and hearing the words of God
We must seek to acquire it
Then manifest it in our hearts
When Satan challenged Jesus Christ
Over two thousand years ago
He fought him not with a sword or blade
But by quoting scriptures from the "word" that we know
But just hearing the "Word" is not quite good enough
It's only just a start, we must hear and acknowledge it
And then engraft it in our hearts

Dare to Be Different

As we become new Christians
Trying hard to do our best
We must dare to be different
So we may stand out from all the rest
We may become mounted with temptation
As we go from day to day
For Satan is always out there
Hoping we would fall into his prey

We must dare to be different every minute of the day
And continuously ask God's guidance
As we go along the way
For the world is constantly watching us
As we go the whole day through
We must dare to be different
So that others can see Christ's goodness in you

The Comforter

When life's problems are getting you down and
you don't know which way to go
When your health has drastically deteriorated and
your finances are very, very low.
Take heed in knowing that there is a comforter
who will supply your every need
you must first go to him and ask him
have faith and believe.
When your job situation is problematic and your
chances for a promotion is lessening every day
just go to God in all sincerity and he will help you
find a way.
When your friends and family put you down and
a solution seems impossible to acquire
just ask God to help you and he will fulfill your
heart's desire.
During your trials and tribulations God still loves you so
but he allows you to experience them in order to develop and
grow.
So when you experience certain problems in your struggles
from day to day
just ask God to spearhead and direct the situation
and he will show you a way.

Lord, Make Me a Christian

Lord make me a Christian
And come into my heart today
Strengthen me in my daily quest
So that I might never stray
Lord make me a Christian, fill my mind with your word
So that I may be equipped to fight Satan with an armor
And a double-edge sword
Lord make me a Christian and
Lead me on the path that I should go
Help me become a good foot soldier
To spread your word to and fro
Cushion me when I fall
Support me when I am weak
Keep my eyes focused on you
And place a lamp unto my feet
Lord help me become a Christian
As I go from day to day
And as I travel life's journey, Lord
Help me remember to pray
Purge and cleanse me from
My head to my feet
So that when my time here has ended
You and I both shall meet

My Prayer

Lord I'm not perfect
And do not live like I ought
But when I'm overly critical of others
Lord help me to see my own faults
Help me to analyze my actions
And look at these old faults that I possess
And give me the strength to change them so
That I might have less and less

Help me Lord to realize that these faults
Did not just come on overnight
So it's going to take more than one night
To decrease them in thy sight
Lord give me the skills to overcome these old negative faults
of mine and a sincere desire to change them
Within a given amount of time

Onward Christian Soldiers

Onward Christian Soldiers
As we march off to war
With a silver plated armor
The Bible and a double-edged sword
Our mission is to win other souls for Christ
As we teach God's word far and near
Our goal is to spread Christianity
To our families and friends
Whom we hold so dear

We must make soldiers out of the common man
As we fight daily battles for Christ
Pledging to keep him as our leader
As we strive to lead a more spiritual
And rewarding life
So onward we march soldiers,
As we fight daily wars
Never tiring, never ceasing continuously marching
1234...1234...1234...1234.

Buckle up for Safety

In this wicked world of ours
As we go from day to day
We occasionally forget to buckle up for safety
Allowing Satan to have his way

We fail to put on the whole Armor of God
Giving Satan that added edge
To penetrate our bodies
For the lack of a protective hedge

The "word" tells us to put on a protective shield
As we go throughout the day
So we can be fully protected
As Satan tries to have his way

As we begin another day
After kneeling down to pray
We should buckle up for safety
Equipping ourselves with a greater protective device
So that we might have a safer and better day

A New Convert

A new convert will never forget the day
When Christ entered his life
Cleansed him and washed his sins away
Once you're washed with the blood
You become a new person in Christ
You must stay on the path and
Continue to do all the things that are right
You will take on the "new man"
As the "old man" is cast aside
Bringing new hopes, dreams, and attitudes as
You take on the Holy Spirit as your guide
Once you become a Christian, God gives you a brand new life
Old things are cast aside in the sea and forgotten
As you strive for a greater relationship with Jesus Christ
Contrary to your life in the world
Where old things are remembered by all
Some people will remind you from time to time
In hopes that you may fall
But God's word will remind you to press onward toward the mark
And to do all the things that are right
The end result as you well know, is to share paradise with
our Lord and Savior Jesus Christ

Believe in God

When your health is not what it used to be
When pain and suffering are always near
Believe in God to see you through all this
For he knows just how much you can bear
When family problems are overbearing
And the healing process seems very slow
Believe in God to help you get past all this
And he will show you which way to go

When your enemies have you out numbered
And there is no place to run or hide
Believe in God to fight your battles
For he is always right there, by your side
When your bills are at an all-time high
And your finances are at an all-time low
Believe in God to see you through all this
For he is the best financial planner I know

God is Alive

God is alive today and not dead as some perceive
He wants us to trust and obey him
Do his will and believe
God is not dead, he's very much alive
Evidence of this can be seen all around us
As we go on with our lives

He will give us needed comfort
And cushion us when we fall
Place a hedge of protection all around us
As we bear life's daily turmoil

God is not dead and his mercy
Graciously endures
As he patiently allows us the opportunity
To change our lifestyle and to seriously improve

Trust in Jesus

It's good to put your trust in Jesus
As you go from day to day
For he will help you through life's hurdles
And will clearly show you the way
It's good to put your trust in Jesus
As you weather through the storm
For He will comfort you when needed
And give you the strength to go on

It's good to put your trust in Jesus
As you face life's biggest test
Just in simple faith, trust him
And he will give you his very best
It's good to put your trust in Jesus
As you go from day to day
The Bible clearly tells us
"If you want to be happy in Jesus
You must trust him and obey"

You Are the Potter, I Am the Clay

In your quest to make me better Lord
And in my will to obey
Continuously bring to my remembrance
That you are the potter and I am the clay
If by chance I begin to malfunction
Or to seriously go astray
Break me and start at the beginning
Just go on and have your way
Turn up the furnace all the way with the heat
So that I might be baked inside out
After forming me with your heart's desire
Take away all my fears and doubts
Once I'm fully baked and become solid and strong
Lord guide my path daily
So that I might do no wrong
As my faith in you is strengthened
And I go from day to day
Help me to remember dear Lord
That you are indeed the potter
And I am just a mere piece of clay

Insight

The Apostle Paul had wisdom far beyond his years
He rejoiced greatly in the Lord
Then thanked Him daily through his prayers
He learned the secret of peace and joy
And shared it willingly with folks far and near
He shared strategies and techniques
For everyday problems, and encouraged others to be content
For whatever circumstances your life has to bear
For he knew what it was to be in need
And he knew what it meant to have plenty
He learned the secret of being content whether well fed
Living in abundance or hungry without having a penny
This secret he learned was therapeutic
And can be yours without paying a mint
It is realizing that you too can do anything through Christ
For it is He, who gives you strength

To Purchase additional copies of this book please visit.

www.AWalkThroughLifesGarden.com
Like us on Facebook!
Twitter.com/AWalkThroughLG
Instagram.com/AWalkThroughLG
Email: AWalkThroughLifesGarden@Gmail.com

www.ingramcontent.com/pod-product-compliance
Lightning Source LLC
Chambersburg PA
CBHW051711040426
42446CB00008B/826